Peter Mohrs

Mein erstes Konzert

My First Concert

22 leichte Vortragsstücke aus 5 Jahrhunderten
22 Easy Concert Pieces from 5 Centuries

für Violine und Klavier
for Violin and Piano

ED 22069
ISMN 979-0-001-20161-2

www.schott-music.com

Mainz · London · Berlin · Madrid · New York · Paris · Prague · Tokyo · Toronto
© 2015 SCHOTT MUSIC GmbH & Co. KG, Mainz · Printed in Germany

Impressum:

Bestellnummer: ED 22069
ISMN 979-0-001-20161-2
ISBN 978-3-7957-4958-3

Cover: Katharina, 13 Jahre (Foto: Peter Mohrs)
BSS 56631 · Printed in Germany

Inhalt / Contents

Vorwort

Das Heft *Mein erstes Konzert* enthält 22 leichte Stücke für Violine und Klavier. Es wendet sich an Geigerinnen und Geiger, die schon einmal erste „richtige" Stücke spielen möchten und geeignete Literatur für Musikschulkonzerte, Vorspiele und Schülerwettbewerbe suchen.

Mit dem Band erlebt man eine musikalische Reise durch fünf Epochen: beginnend bei der Renaissance, über Barock, Klassik und Romantik bis hin zur Musik der Gegenwart. Es war mir ein Anliegen, zum Schluss genügend Raum für Popularmusik zu geben. So findet man dort motivierende – und größtenteils eigens für dieses Heft komponierte – Stücke aus den Bereichen Pop, Jazz, Spiritual, Bossa nova und Tango.

Einige Werke sind bereits nach zwei Unterrichtsjahren spielbar. Es wurden aber bewusst auch etwas anspruchsvollere ausgesucht, die dann im Laufe des weiteren Unterrichts erarbeitet werden können. Der Violinlehrer wird schnell erkennen, ob die Stücke für seine Schülerinnen und Schüler den richtigen Schwierigkeitsgrad haben. Noch leichtere Literatur findet man in meinem Heft *Klassik für Kinder*, das ebenfalls bei Schott Music erschienen ist (ED 20684).

Der überwiegende Teil der Kompositionen sind Originalwerke, die die Kenntnis aller vier Griffarten verlangen und in der 1. Lage spielbar sind. Bei einer Komposition, die das Lagenspiel erfordert, wurde eine leichtere Alternative hinzugefügt. Die Stücke können selbstverständlich vom Lehrer auch mit Lagen-Fingersätzen eingerichtet werden, um das klangliche Ergebnis zu verbessern.

Viele der Klavierbegleitungen sind für fortgeschrittene Schülerinnen und Schüler geeignet und fördern somit das gemeinschaftliche Musizieren.

Nun wünsche ich viel Spaß beim Spielen und eine spannende Reise durch 400 Jahre Violinmusik.

Peter Mohrs

Preface

My First Concert contains 22 easy pieces for violin and piano. It is intended for violinists who are keen to play 'proper' pieces and looking for suitable repertoire for school concerts, auditions and competitions.

This book offers a musical journey through five different eras starting with the Renaissance, through Baroque, Classical and Romantic eras to the music of today. I was keen to find enough space at the end for popular music, so there are inspiring examples of pop, jazz, spirituals, bossa nova and tango – most of them composed especially for this book.

Some of these pieces should be playable after two years of tuition. More challenging music has deliberately been included too, though, for working on as lessons progress. The violin teacher will quickly be able to identify pieces at the right level for their pupils. Even easier pieces will be found in my book *Classical Music for Children*, also published by Schott Music (ED 20684).

The majority of these compositions are original works using all fingering patterns in first position. One composition that includes position changes also gives an easier alternative version. The teacher could mark in position changes, of course, for more expressive playing.

Many of the piano accompaniments are suitable for advanced students, encouraging children to enjoy playing pieces together.

Now have fun playing on an exciting journey through four hundred years of violin music!

Peter Mohrs
Translation Julia Rushworth

I. Renaissance
Pavane

Luis Milán
(ca. 1500–1561)
Basso continuo: Wolfgang Birtel

II. Barock / Baroque
Air

Gottfried Finger
(ca.1660 – ca.1730)
B.c.: Erich Doflein

8

Un peu gay

François Duval
(1672–1728)
B.c.: Hugo Ruf

*) Achtel staccato / quavers staccato

aus / from: F. Duval, Sonate Nr. 1 in D-Dur, Schott ANT 33

Largo

Georg Philipp Telemann
(1681–1767)
B.c.: Erich Doflein

aus / from: G. Ph. Telemann, 6 Sonaten für Violine und B.c. / 6 Sonatas for Violin and B.c., Schott ED 4221

Allegro ma moderato

Gottfried Kirchhoff
(1685–1746)
Arr.: Walter Serauky

*) Original:

aus / from: G. Kirchhoff, Sonaten für Violine und Klavier, Bd. 2 / Sonatas for Violin and Piano, Vol. 2, Schott ED 5061

D. C. al Fine

III. Klassik / Classical Age

Rondo

Ignaz Pleyel
(1757–1831)
Arr.: Gustav Lenzewski

nach / after: I. Pleyel, 6 leichte Duette für 2 Violinen / 6 Easy Duets for 2 Violins, op. 8, Schott ED 673

Aus wendetechnischen Gründen bleibt diese Seite frei.
This page is left blank to save an unnecessary turn.

Un Ballo

Daniel Steibelt
(1765 – 1823)
Arr.: Alfred Moffat

Allegro, ma non tanto ♪ ca. 132

IV. Romantik / Romantic Age

Rondo

Charles Dancla
(1817–1907)

aus / from: Ch. Dancla, Kleine Melodien-Schule / Little School of Melody, op.123, Schott ED 749

Andante

Edward Elgar
(1857–1934)

aus / from: 6 sehr leichte Stücke / 6 Very Easy Pieces, op. 22

Der Spaßvogel / The Jester

Alexander Gretchaninoff
(1864–1956)
Arr.: T. S. Walker

Allegro moderato ♩ ca. 104

V. Moderne / Modern Age

Andante

Carl Orff
(1895–1982)
Arr.: Hermann Regner

aus / from: C. Orff, Orff-Schulwerk, Flötenbuch / Recorder Book, Schott ED 9248

Spiellied / Playsong

Carl Orff
Arr.: Hermann Regner

*) mit der linken Hand auf den Schenkel schlagen / slap your thigh with the left hand

aus / from: C. Orff, Orff-Schulwerk, Flötenbuch / Recorder Book, Schott ED 9248

Spiritual

Eduard Pütz
(1911–2000)
Arr.: Peter Mohrs

aus / from: E. Pütz, Short Stories, 10 Easy Pieces for Cello and Piano, Schott ED 7533

Lalai
Schlaflied zum Wachwerden?
A Lullaby to awaken you?

Barbara Heller
(*1936)

aus / from: B. Heller, Lalai – Schlaflied zum Wachwerden? für Violine und Klavier, Schott VLB 149

Inhalt / Contents

I. Renaissance
Pavane

Luis Milán
(ca. 1500–1561)

II. Barock / Baroque
Air

Gottfried Finger
(ca.1660 – ca.1730)

Un peu gay

François Duval
(1672–1728)

*) Achtel staccato / quavers staccato

aus / from: F. Duval, Sonate Nr. 1 in D-Dur, Schott ANT 33

Largo

Georg Philipp Telemann
(1681–1767)

4

aus / from: G. Ph. Telemann, 6 Sonaten für Violine und B.c. / 6 Sonatas for Violin and B.c., Schott ED 4221

Allegro ma moderato

Gottfried Kirchhoff
(1685–1746)

5

aus / from: G. Kirchhoff, Sonaten für Violine und Klavier, Bd. 2 / Sonatas for Violin and Piano, Vol. 2, Schott ED 5061

Fine

D. C. al Fine

*) Original:

III. Klassik / Classical Age

Rondo

Ignaz Pleyel
(1757–1831)

nach / after: I. Pleyel, 6 leichte Duette für 2 Violinen / 6 Easy Duets for 2 Violins, op. 8, Schott ED 673

Aus wendetechnischen Gründen bleibt diese Seite frei.
This page is left blank to save an unnecessary turn.

Un Ballo

Daniel Steibelt
(1765 – 1823)

Allegro, ma non tanto ♪ ca. 132

IV. Romantik / Romantic Age

Rondo

Charles Dancla
(1817–1907)

aus / from: Ch. Dancla, Kleine Melodien-Schule / Little School of Melody, op.123, Schott ED 749

Andante

Edward Elgar
(1857–1934)

aus / from: 6 sehr leichte Stücke / 6 Very Easy Pieces, op. 22

Der Spaßvogel / The Jester

V. Moderne / Modern Age

Andante

aus / from: C. Orff, Orff-Schulwerk, Flötenbuch / Recorder Book, Schott ED 9248

Spiellied / Playsong

Carl Orff

Spiritual

Eduard Pütz
(1911–2000)

aus / from: E. Pütz, Short Stories, 10 Easy Pieces for Cello and Piano, Schott ED 7533

Lalai

Schlaflied zum Wachwerden?
A Lullaby to awaken you?

Barbara Heller
(*1936)

aus / from: B. Heller, Lalai – Schlaflied zum Wachwerden? für Violine und Klavier, Schott VLB 149

VI. Pop, Jazz, Tango und mehr... / Pop, Jazz, Tango and more...

Abenddämmerung / Evening Twilight

Jürgen Moser
(*1949)

aus / from: J. Moser, Let's Play Together, Schott ED 20404

Fips in the Park

Mike Schoenmehl
(*1957)

Princess Sivama's Song

Peter Mohrs
(*1956)

Windlied / Windsong

Gabriel Koeppen
(*1958)

Chill-Out

Gabriel Koeppen
(*1958)

Like a Bird

Daniel Kemminer
(*1978)

D. C. al Fine

Un sueño truncado
Unerfüllter Traum / Unfilled Dream

Daniel Kemminer
(*1978)

Song for Friends

Peter Mohrs

VI. Pop, Jazz, Tango und mehr… / Pop, Jazz, Tango and more…

Abenddämmerung / Evening Twilight

Jürgen Moser
(*1949)

Fips in the Park

Mike Schoenmehl
(*1957)

Princess Sivama's Song

Peter Mohrs
(*1956)

Windlied / Windsong

Gabriel Koeppen
(*1958)

Chill-Out

Gabriel Koeppen
(*1958)

Like a Bird

Daniel Kemminer
(*1978)

D. C. al Fine

Un sueño truncado
Unerfüllter Traum / Unfilled Dream

Daniel Kemminer
(*1978)

Aus wendetechnischen Gründen bleibt diese Seite frei.
This page is left blank to save an unnecessary turn.

46

Song for Friends

Peter Mohrs
(*1956)

Über die Komponisten

Luis Milán (ca. 1500–ca. 1561)

Spanischer Renaissance-Komponist und Vihuelaspieler (die Vihuela ist ein gitarreähnliches Instrument). Seine Musik ist heute vor allem bei klassischen Gitarristen beliebt, weil sie einfach für dieses Instrument bearbeitet werden kann. Einige Stücke eignen sich aber auch sehr gut für eine Übertragung auf Streichinstrumente. So z.B. die hier vorliegende *Pavane*, ein geradtaktiger, einfacher Schreittanz spanisch-italienischer Herkunft, der im 16./17. Jahrhundert in ganz Europa verbreitet war.

Gottfried Finger (ca. 1660–ca. 1730)

Der Barockkomponist Gottfried Finger, geboren in Olmütz (Mähren), wirkte lange Zeit in England. Zuerst ab 1685 in der königlichen Kapelle, später mit Erfolg als freischaffender und anerkannter Künstler im Londoner Musikleben. Nach 1702 hatte er verschiedene Stellungen in Berlin, Innsbruck und Gotha inne, bis er um 1730 in Mannheim starb. Die leicht spielbare *Air* (= *Lied* oder *Melodie*) ist original für Blockflöte geschrieben.

François Duval (1672–1728)

Der französischer Geiger und Komponist François Duval war Mitglied der „24 Streicher des Königs" am französischen Hof in Schloss Versailles. Zu diesem Ensemble zählten so namhafte Musiker wie Jean-Marie Leclair, Jean-Baptiste Lully und Jacques Aubert. Der vorliegende Satz aus einer Violinsonate ist überschrieben mit *Un peu gay*, was man mit *etwas fröhlich* übersetzen kann. Unter *Croches piquées* versteht man *gestoßene Achtel*, die in etwa einem *staccato* entsprechen. Das Zeichen + fordert eine Verzierung, die man – je nach Leistungsstand oder Geschmack – mit einem Triller oder einem Praller füllen kann.

Georg Philipp Telemann (1681–1767)

Telemann ist neben J.S. Bach, G. Fr. Händel und A. Vivaldi einer der wichtigsten und bekanntesten barocken Komponisten. Er wurde in Magdeburg geboren und wirkte zunächst als Musikdirektor und Kirchenmusiker in Frankfurt, später als Leiter der „Oper am Gänsemarkt" in Hamburg. Telemanns melodischer Stil gab der Musik des 18. Jahrhunderts neue Impulse. Hervorzuheben ist, dass er in seinen Kompositionen zumeist kein Interesse an besonders virtuosem Instrumentalspiel zeigte. Er schrieb vieles bewusst in geringerem technischem Schwierigkeitsgrad, was ihn für die Streicherausbildung besonders wichtig werden lässt. Sein *Largo* (largo = langsam, breit) aus einer Sonate für Violine und Basso continuo ist ein gesangliches Stück, das „Wanderstrich" und eine gute Kontaktstellenarbeit erfordert.

Gottfried Kirchhoff (1685–1746)

1685 wurden nicht nur die berühmten barocken Komponisten J. S. Bach und G. Fr. Händel geboren, sondern auch der recht unbekannte Organist und Komponist Kirchhoff. Der vorliegende Satz entstammt einem Zyklus von zwölf Sonaten für Violine und Basso continuo, der – wie auch die Sonaten von J. C. Pepusch – die Lücke zwischen einfachen barocken Tänzen und Spielstücken zu den technisch anspruchsvolleren Sonaten von Händel und Bach schließt. Das *Allegro ma moderato* enthält sehr schöne motorische Passagen, deren Laufwerk an die schnellen Sätze Vivaldis erinnert.

Ignaz Pleyel (1757–1831)

Österreichischer Komponist der Klassik, lebte später in Paris als Klavierfabrikant und Musikverleger und erhielt später die französische Staatsbürgerschaft. Er war Schüler J. Haydns und J. B. Vanhals. Pleyel hinterließ zahlreiche Kompositionen, welche damals an Beliebtheit selbst mit denen Haydns wetteifern konnten und von Mozart geschätzt wurden. Den Geigern hat er zahlreiche Duette unterschiedlichen Schwierigkeitsgrades hinterlassen. Das hier ausgewählte gefällige *Rondo* ist eine Bearbeitung aus den Violinduetten op. 8.

Daniel Steibelt (1765–1823)

Deutscher Pianist und Komponist der Klassik, geboren in Berlin, wirkte später in Paris und London. Steibelt war einer der geschäftstüchtigsten und produktivsten Komponisten seiner Zeit und schrieb Opern, Klavierkonzerte und -sonaten, Kammermusik und zahlreiche Violinsonaten – Werke, die heute allerdings kaum noch bekannt sind. Die Komposition *Un Ballo* ist ein heiteres Werk in Rondoform, das wie die Wiener Sonatine dem rechten Arm schon einiges abverlangt.

Charles Dancla (1817–1907)

Der französische Violinvirtuose wirkte in Paris als Sologeiger an der Oper. Neben J. F. Mazas gehörte er zu den wenigen romantischen Komponisten, deren Werke einen oft pädagogischen Hintergrund besitzen. Er schrieb neben mehreren Bänden einer Violinschule u.a. eine Duoschule, zahlreiche Etüden sowie Kammermusik. Seine *École de la mélodie (Schule der Melodie)* ist heute noch ein weit verbreitetes Unterrichtswerk, aus dem das vorliegende Rondo ausgewählt wurde. Beachtenswert sind für Geigerinnen und Geiger auch die *36 Études mélodiques et faciles, op. 84*, die bei Schott als Neuauflage erschienen sind (ED 21126). Das hier vorliegende hübsche *Rondo* enthält in seinen vielen gebundenen Sechzehntelläufen schon einige schwierigere Grifkombinationen und gehört zu den technisch anspruchsvolleren Stücken des Heftes.

Edward Elgar (1857–1934)

Neben Henry Purcell und Benjamin Britten gehört der Romantiker Elgar zu den herausragenden Komponisten Englands. Bekannt wurde er u.a. durch das Orchesterstück „Pomp and Circumstances", das traditionsgemäß bei Hochzeiten des englischen Königshauses gespielt wird. Elgar verdanken wir mit den *Six very easy Pieces op. 22* für Violine und Klavier wichtige Originalstücke: Sechs leichte romantische Miniaturen, von denen hier der erste Satz *Andante* ausgewählt wurde. Es ist ein sehr leichtes Werk, das an die linke Hand kaum Anforderungen stellt, sodass man sich gut auf den rechten Arm konzentrieren kann, dem die Gestaltung eines Stückes obliegt.

Alexander Gretchaninoff (1864–1956)

Der russisch-amerikanische Komponist und Dirigent, geboren in Moskau, gestorben in New York, studierte u.a. bei N. Rimskij-Korsakow. 1925 ließ er sich in Paris nieder und ging 1939 nach Amerika. Er schrieb über 200 Werke, von denen vor allem die Kinderstücke für verschiedene Besetzungen sowie Kinderopern populär wurden. Bei dem Stück *Der Spaßvogel / The Jester* sollte man sich bemühen, den witzigen Charakter herauszuarbeiten. Dabei helfen die genaue Befolgung der Dynamik ebenso wie eine kurze Artikulation (Staccato) bei den Achtelnoten. Wenn man dann noch die Akzente in den Takten 1, 2, 5, 6 u.a. ganz laut mit der leeren A-Saite spielt, schaut aus dem Stück deutlich ein kleiner Clown heraus...

Carl Orff (1895–1982)

geboren in München, deutscher Komponist und Musikpädagoge. Er gründete in den 1930er Jahren eine eigene Musikschule zusammen mit Gunild Keetman, in der es ihm um Musikerziehung durch Tanz, Bewegung und Improvisation ging. Dazu entwickelte er eigene Schlaginstrumente, die noch heute als sog. „Orff-Instrumente" bekannt sind und in allen Schulen stehen. Sein bekanntestes Werk ist die szenische Kantate *Carmina Burana*, die zu einem der populärsten Chorwerke des 20. Jahrhunderts wurde. Die beiden ausgewählten Stücke stammen aus seiner gemeinsam mit Gunild Keetman entwickelten fünfbändigen Sammlung „Musik für Kinder". Die vorliegende Fassung wurde von seinem Schüler Hermann Regner bearbeitet.

Eduard Pütz (1911–2000)

geboren in Illerich/Eifel, studierte Schulmusik und Mathematik an der Musikhochschule und Universität Köln. Er wirkte als Lehrer an einem Gymnasium in Rheinbach bei Bonn sowie als Dozent für Musiktheorie an der Rheinischen Musikschule in Köln. Pütz schrieb bewusst viele leichte Stücke für Musikschüler, da er als Lehrer die pädagogische Praxis unmittelbar vor Augen hatte. Er baut Brücken zwischen der so genannten E-Musik und der U-Musik und verbindet somit die Klassische Musik mit Jazz und Unterhaltungsmusik. Sein *Spiritual*, ursprünglich für Cello und Klavier komponiert, hat eine schlichte, aber sehr ausdrucksstarke Melodie und ist den geistlichen Liedern nachempfunden, die die farbigen Sklaven Amerikas im 19. Jahrhundert sangen.

Barbara Heller (*1936)

lebt als Komponistin und Pianistin in Darmstadt. Als Herausgeberin widmete sie sich besonders den Werken von Komponistinnen, die sie in der Reihe „Frauen komponieren" im Verlag Schott veröffentlicht. In dem Stück *Lalai* greift Heller auf ein iranisches Lied zurück. Es ist 50 iranischen Frauen gewidmet, die 1989 im Evin-Gefängnis in Teheran umgebracht wurden. Für das vorliegende Heft wurde nur das Thema des Werkes in einer etwas erleichterten Fassung ausgewählt. Das Originalwerk enthält einige technisch anspruchsvolle Variationen über dieses Thema.

Jürgen Moser (*1949)

Der Klavierpädagoge, Musiker, Komponist und Autor arbeitete viele Jahre als Musikschullehrer in Rüsselsheim. Mit verschiedenen Rock-, Blues- und Jazzbands gab er Konzerte und sammelte Bühnenerfahrung. Sein Lehrbuch „Rock Piano" ist eines der Standardwerke für den Klavierunterricht. Ausgewählt wurde hier eine Originalkomposition aus dem Heft *Let's play together,* deren Melodie mit den einfühlsamen Harmonien im Klavier eine sehr schöne Abendstimmung malt.

Mike Schoenmehl (*1957)

Schoenmehl studierte Musikerziehung an der Universität Mainz. Er unterrichtet Klavier, Jazzharmonielehre und Improvisation, seit 1986 als Dozent an der Frankfurter Musikwerkstatt (FMW), seit 1995 an der Hochschule für Musik und Darstellende Kunst in Frankfurt. Außerdem hat er seit 1996 einen Lehrauftrag für Jazzpiano an der Universität Mainz. Seine Komposition *Fips in the Park*, ursprünglich für Klavier vierhändig komponiert, ist mit ihrer eingängigen Melodik und den herrlichen Jazzakkorden auch für Violine und Klavier ein echter „Ohrwurm". Die Achtel sind ternär (= triolisch) zu spielen, also mit Swing-Feeling.

Peter Mohrs (*1956)

studierte Instrumentalpädagogik an der Musikhochschule Saarbrücken und der Universität Koblenz-Landau. Seit 1979 unterrichtet er an der Musikschule des Landkreises Bernkastel-Wittlich die Fächer Violine, Viola und Kammermusik. Für seine Musikschularbeit schreibt er Stücke unterschiedlichster Art für junge Streicher. Sein *Princess Sivama's Song* ist eine Hommage an eine Prinzessin aus dem fernen Orient. *Song for Friends* ist allen kleinen und großen Geigenliebhabern gewidmet.

Gabriel Koeppen (*1958)

Der Cellist, Saxophonist und Komponist ist Leiter der Musikschule in Flensburg. Er ist Verfasser einer Celloschule und komponierte zahlreiche Stücke für Cello von ganz leicht bis sehr anspruchsvoll. Dabei bedient er sich der Tonsprache von Blues, Pop, Tango, Rock und vielem mehr. Darüber hinaus ist er Dozent an der Universität Flensburg und leitet Workshops und Fortbildungen. Bei dem schwungvollen *Windlied / Windsong* (original für Cello und Klavier) braucht man eine sehr bewegliche Bogeneinteilung und in dem munteren *Chill-Out* ist manche rhythmische Nuss zu knacken.

Daniel Kemminer (*1978)

Nach seinem Studium an der Musikhochschule in Köln arbeitet Kemminer als Musiklehrer an einem Gymnasium. Als Sänger wirkte er in verschiedenen Opernproduktionen mit und ist Gründungsmitglied des Ensembles für Neue Musik *Garage und gRoBA*. Als Pianist ist er im Kabarett- und Pop-Bereich tätig. Er schrieb zahlreiche Arrangements und Kompositionen für Gesangsensemble und verschiedene Instrumentalbesetzungen. Seine beiden Kompositionen *Un sueño truñcado* und *Like a Bird* sind Originalbeiträge für das vorliegende Heft. Ersteres ist eine Liebeserklärung an den argentinischen Tango, das zweite ein unbekümmert-fröhliches Stück, das sich mit Sicherheit in jedem Ohr festsetzen wird.

About the composers

Luis Milán (c.1500–c.1561)

Music by this Spanish Renaissance composer and vihuela player is particularly popular with classical guitarists, as it can easily be arranged for guitar (the vihuela is an instrument similar to a guitar). Some of his pieces also lend themselves very well to transcription for string instruments – such as the *Pavane* included here, a simple stately dance in duple time of Spanish-Italian origin that was popular all over Europe in the 16th and 17th Centuries.

Gottfried Finger (c.1660–c.1730)

The Baroque composer Gottfried Finger was born in Olmütz (Moravia) and worked in England for a long time. He played at the Chapel Royal from 1685 and later worked as a successful freelance musician in London. After 1702 he held various posts in Berlin, Innsbruck and Gotha; he died in Mannheim in 1730. This easy *Air* was originally written for the recorder.

François Duval (1672–1728)

The French violinist and composer François Duval was a member of 'The King's Twenty-four Strings' at the French court in Versailles, an ensemble that included renowned musicians such as Jean-Marie Leclair, Jean-Baptiste Lully and Jacques Aubert. This movement from a violin sonata is marked at the top *Un peu gay*, which could be translated as 'rather jolly'. *Croches piquées* are taken to mean accented quavers, something like a *staccato*. The sign + calls for an ornament – either a trill or mordent, according to the player's ability or preference.

Georg Philipp Telemann (1681–1767)

Telemann is one of the most significant and best-known Baroque composers besides J. S. Bach, G. F. Handel and A. Vivaldi. He was born in Magdeburg and worked as a director of music and church musician in Frankfurt; later on he was conductor of the Opera at the Goose Market in Hamburg. Telemann's melodic style brought new impetus to the music of the eighteenth Century. It is worth noting that he generally showed no interest in special displays of virtuoso instrumental technique in his compositions. He wrote many pieces with deliberately modest technical demands, making his music particularly valuable for aspiring string players. His *Largo* (*largo* = slow, broad) comes from a sonata for violin and continuo bass: it is a lyrical piece that requires the use of varying lengths of bow, with a focus on good bow contact.

Gottfried Kirchhoff (1685–1746)

The celebrated Baroque composers J. S. Bach and G. F. Handel were both born in 1685 – as was Kirchhoff, a little-known organist and composer. This movement comes from a cycle of twelve sonatas for violin and continuo bass – like the sonatas of J. C. Pepusch, it fills the gap between simple Baroque pieces or dances and the technically more demanding sonatas of Handel and Bach. This *Allegro ma moderato* includes some lovely passages in a motor-like rhythm with rapid sequences reminiscent of fast movements by Vivaldi.

Ignaz Pleyel (1757–1831)

This Austrian composer of the classical period spent the latter part of his life in Paris as a piano manufacturer and music publisher, eventually acquiring French citizenship. He was a pupil of J. Haydn and J. B. Vanhals. Pleyel wrote numerous pieces praised by Mozart and, in their day, almost as popular as music by Haydn. For violinists he wrote many duets of varying degrees of difficulty. The *Rondo* selected here is an arrangement from his Violin Duets Op. 8.

Daniel Steibelt (1765–1823)

This German pianist and composer of the classical period was born in Berlin and later lived in Paris and London. Steibelt was one of the most prolific composers of his day, writing operas, piano concertos and sonatas, chamber music and numerous violin sonatas – yet his music is hardly known today. *Un Ballo* is a jolly composition in rondo form which, like the Viennese Sonatina, makes considerable demands on the right arm.

Charles Dancla (1817–1934)

This French virtuoso violinist was leader of the orchestra at the Paris Opera. Along with J. F. Mazas he is one of the few Romantic composers whose works have some educational method behind them. Besides a violin tutorial method in several volumes he wrote a tutorial book of duos, numerous studies and chamber music too. The *École de la mélodie* from which this Rondo is taken is still used widely used in lessons. Also worth looking at for young violinists are Dancla's *36 Études mélodiques et faciles* Op. 84, published by Schott in a new edition (ED 21126). This pretty *Rondo* includes quite a few tricky combinations of finger positions among its many semiquaver runs and is one of the most technically demanding pieces in this book.

Edward Elgar (1857–1934)

Along with Henry Purcell and Benjamin Britten, the Romantic Elgar is one of England's most distinguished composers. He became known for works such as his orchestral music 'Pomp and Circumstance', traditionally played on great British ceremonial occasions such as royal weddings. Elgar's *Six very easy Pieces* Op. 22 for violin and piano provide us with valuable original pieces in six easy Romantic miniatures from which we have chosen the first movement, *Andante*. It is a very easy piece that places few demands on the left hand, allowing for a focus on the right arm – so important for shaping the music.

Alexander Gretchaninoff (1864–1956)

This Russian-American composer and conductor was born in Moscow, died in New York and studied with N. Rimsky-Korsakov, among others. He went to live in Paris in 1925 and moved to America in 1939. Of Gretchaninoff's compositions - over two hundred works in all – his pieces for children have been particularly popular, including music for various combinations of instruments and children's operas. Efforts should be made to bring out the witty character of *The Jester*: it will be helpful to pay close attention to dynamics and use short articulation (*staccato*) for the quavers. If the accents in bars 1, 2, 5, 6 and so on are played quite loud on an open A string, a little clown will be seen peeping out of the music...

Carl Orff (1895–1982)

This German composer and music educator was born in Munich. In the 1930s he founded his own music school with Gunild Keetman, with an emphasis on musical education through dance, movement and improvisation. To that end he developed his own percussion instruments, still known today as 'Orff instruments' and found in schools all over Germany. His best-known work is the cantata *Carmina Burana*, which became one of the most popular twentieth-Century choral works. The two pieces selected here come from the five-volume collection of 'Music for Children' Orff put together with Gunild Keetman. This version was arranged by his pupil Hermann Regner.

Eduard Pütz (1911–2000)

Born in Illerich on the Eifel, Pütz studied music and mathematics at the Academy of Music and at the University in Cologne. He taught at a grammar school in Rheinbach, near Bonn, and lectured in music theory at the Rhine Academy of Music in Cologne. Pütz purposely wrote many easy pieces for students to play – as a teacher, he was very aware of educational content. He also built bridges between 'serious' and lighter music, bringing classical music together with jazz and light entertainment. His *Spiritual*, originally composed for cello and piano, has a simple yet expressive melody inspired by the spirituals sung by coloured slaves in America in the nineteenth Century.

Barbara Heller (b.1936)

This composer and pianist lives in Darmstadt. As an editor she has focused in particular on works by women composers published by Schott in the series 'Female Composers'. In *Lalai* Heller takes up an Iranian song: it is dedicated to fifty Iranian women killed at Evin prison in Teheran in 1989. For this book the theme of that piece is presented alone in a slightly simplified version; the original work includes some technically demanding variations on this theme.

Jürgen Moser (b.1949)

This piano teacher, performing musician, composer and author taught at a music school in Rüsselsheim for many years. He also gave concerts and made many stage appearances with various rock, blues and jazz bands. 'Rock Piano' is one of the standard works used in piano tuition. Here an original composition has been selected from the book *Let's play together*: its melody and sympathetic harmonies in the piano part evoke a lovely evening mood.

Mike Schoenmehl (b.1957)

Schoenmehl studied music education at Mainz University. He teaches piano, jazz harmony and improvisation, lecturing at The Frankfurt Music Workshop (FMW) since 1986 and at the Frankfurt Academy of Music and Performing Arts since 1995. He has also taught jazz piano at Mainz University since 1996. His composition *Fips in the Park*, originally written for piano duo, is a really memorable tune for violin and piano, too, with its catchy melody and wonderful jazz chords. The quavers should be played as triplets, with a feeling of swing.

Peter Mohrs (b.1956)

Peter Mohrs studied instrumental teaching at Saarbrücken Academy of Music and the University of Koblenz-Landau. He has taught violin, viola and chamber music at the music school serving the district of Bernkastel-Wittlich since 1979. In his role as a music teacher he also writes all kinds of pieces for young string players. *Princess Sivama's Song* pays homage to a princess from the Far East. *Song for Friends* is dedicated to violin-lovers young and old.

Gabriel Koeppen (b.1958)

This cellist, saxophonist and composer is the Director of Flensburg Music School. He is the author of a tutorial method for the cello and has written numerous pieces for the cello, ranging from very easy to very demanding. Koeppen draws on blues, pop, tango, rock and many other musical styles. He also lectures at the University in Flensburg and directs various workshops and courses. His lively *Wind song* (originally for cello and piano) calls for agile and versatile bowing, while his cheerful *Chill-Out* has many a rhythmic nut to crack.

Daniel Kemminer (b.1978)

After completing his studies at the Academy of Music in Cologne Kemminer went to work as a music teacher at a grammar school. As a singer he has been involved in various operatic productions and is a founder member of new music ensembles *Garage* and *gRoBA*. As a pianist he also plays cabaret and pop. Kemminer has written numerous arrangements and original pieces for vocal ensemble and various combinations of instruments. His two compositions *Un sueño truncado* and *Like a Bird* are original compositions for this book: the first is a declaration of love for the Argentinian tango, the second a happy, carefree piece that is bound to catch the attention of every listener.

Unterrichts- und Studienwerke für Violine

Play Along

Die schönsten Volks- und Kinderlieder
für 1-2 Violinen
sehr leicht bearbeitet
Ausgabe mit CD, ED 8798-50
Ausgabe ohne CD, ED 8798

Die schönsten Herbst- und Winterlieder
für 1-2 Violinen
sehr leicht bearbeitet
Ausgabe mit CD, ED 20203-50
Ausgabe ohne CD, ED 20203

Die schönsten Weihnachtslieder
für 1-2 Violinen
sehr leicht bearbeitet
Ausgabe mit CD, ED 8790-50
Ausgabe ohne CD, ED 8790

Folk for Violin
für 1-2 Violinen
herausgegeben von Hans und Marianne Magolt
Ausgabe mit CD, ED 9427

Swinging Folksongs For Violin
Bekannte Folksongs neu bearbeitet
für Violine und Klavier (Klavierstimme zum Ausdrucken), leicht angejazzt und mit Elementen der Popmusik versetzt.
Ausgabe mit CD, ED 20128

Baroque Play-Along
12 bekannte Barockstücke mit authentischen Orchester-Playbacks
Ausgabe mit CD, ED 13156

Swinging Baroque Play-Along
12 Stücke aus dem Barock in einfachen Swing-Arrangements
Ausgabe mit CD, ED 12963

Swinging Classical Play-Along
12 klassische Werke neu bearbeitet
Ausgabe mit CD, ED 13101

Swinging Romantic Play-Along
12 Stücke aus der Romantik in einfachen Swing-Arrangements
Ausgabe mit CD, ED 13095

Movie Themes For Violin
12 unvergessliche Melodien aus den größten Filmen aller Zeiten
Ausgabe mit CD, ED 12976

Christmas Pop For Violin
18 Christmas-Hits für 1-2 Violinen
Inhalt: Feliz Navidad - Wonderful Christmas Time - Winter Wonderland - Mary's Boy Child - Oh my Lord - Mistletoe and Wine - We Wish You a Merry Christmas - Jingle Bells u. a.
Ausgabe mit CD, ED 9720

Etüden

Charles Dancla
Kleine Melodienschule, op. 123
Band 1/2/3
ED 748/749/750

Jakob Dont
Etüden und Capricen, op. 35
ED 6117

Merrick Hildebrandt
Technik des Bogens
SF 5320

Hilmar Höckner
Violin-Übung am Volkslied
Ein Beitrag zur Methodik des elementaren Violinunterrichts
B 121

Heinrich Ernst Kayser
36 Etüden, op. 20
ED 4976

John Kember
Vom-Blatt-Spiel auf der Geige
Eine erfrischend neue Methode
Band 1, ED 12836
Band 2, ED 12837

Pierre Rode
24 Capricen
in Etüdenform in den 24 Tonarten
ED 6512

Arthur Seybold
Die leichtesten Etüden
für den ersten Violin-Unterricht
Heft 1/2
ED 2471/72

Hans Sitt
100 Etüden, op. 32
Heft 1-5
EES 121-125

20 Studien, op. 69
ED 7753

Tonleiterstudien, op. 41
in Doppelgriffen (Terzen, Sexten, Oktaven, Dezimen) zum praktischen Gebrauch
EES 185

2 Violinen

Renate Bruce-Weber
Das fröhliche Weihnachtsheft
Die schönsten Weihnachtslieder aus aller Welt für 2-3 Violinen
ED 7888

Willem de Fesch
Drei leichte Sonaten
ED 4386

(Erich Doflein, Hrsg.)
Frohes Duospiel
Kleine leichte Duos der klassischen Zeit
(1. Lage)
ED 3760

Féréol Mazas
Zwölf kleine Duos, op. 38
Heft 1/2
ED 667/8

Leopold Mozart
Zwölf Spielstücke
ED 4136

Wolfgang Amadeus Mozart
Die Wiener Sonatinen
ED 2220

(Erich Doflein, Hrsg.)
Spielmusik für Violine
Eine Sammlung zum Spiel auf zwei Violinen für Unterricht und Hausmusik
Hindemith
14 leichte Stücke
ED 2211
Hindemith
Kanonische Vortragsstücke und kanonische Variationen
ED 2212
Neue Musik
Neue Violin-Duos von Hindemith, Bartók, Reutter, Orff und Kadosa
ED 6590
Pepping
Variationen und Suite
ED 2218
Ungarische Komponisten
(Seiber, Bartók, Kadosa)
ED 2213

(Paul Bormann, Hrsg.)
Violinduette der Frühklassik
Band 1/2
ED 4385/5052

3 Violinen

Henk Badings
Trio-Cosmos
Heft 1-16
VLB 53-64, 68, 69, 71, 72

Renate Bruce-Weber
Das fröhliche Weihnachtsheft
Die schönsten Weihnachtslieder aus aller Welt für 2-3 Violinen
ED 7888

Erich und Elma Doflein
Das Geigenschulwerk
Fortschreitende Stücke für drei Geigen
Band 1-3
ED 4756/4757/5160

Harald Genzmer
Spielbuch
ED 2753

Violine und Klavier

(Alfred Moffat, Hrsg.)
Alte Meister für junge Spieler
36 leichte klassische Stücke
Band 1-3
ED 844/1553/1619

Béla Bartók
Kinderstücke
ED 4398

Renate Bruce-Weber
Die fröhliche Violine
22 leichte Lieder und Stücke
Spielbuch, ED 20357

Simon Le Duc
Vier Sonaten
Band 1
op. 4/1, op. 4/6
ED 4708
Band 2
op. 1/1, op. 4/4
ED 4709

Alfred Moffat
Sechs leichte Stücke
in der ersten Lage
ED 849

Wolfgang Amadeus Mozart
Eine kleine Nachtmusik
ED 1599

Sonaten
Wiener Urtext Edition
Band 1-3
UT 50032/33/34

(Erich und Elma Doflein, Hrsg.)
Musik für Violine und Klavier
Eine Sammlung progressiv geordnet
Band 1
50 kleine Stücke für Anfänger
ED 6026
Band 2
Leichte Violinstücke verschiedener Art
ED 6027
Band 3
Von Vivaldi bis Viotti
ED 6028
Band 4
Duos bis zur klassischen Sonate
ED 6029

Franz Schubert
Sonaten
op. 137 (D-Dur / D 384 · a-Moll / D 385 · g-Moll / D 408), op. 162 (A-Dur / D 574)
Wiener Urtext Edition
UT 50004

Hans Sitt
Concertino - Moll, op. 93
in der 1. Lage
EES 183

www.schott-music.com